A LIFE OF TRIUMPH

Duane Hickler (signature)

A LIFE OF TRIUMPH

*How a Girl with Cerebral Palsy
Beat the Odds to Achieve Success*

By Karen A. Gorr
as told to Duane Hickler

CNM Press

TABLE OF CONTENTS

INTRODUCTION

My mother's brother, Duane Hickler (or, as I like to call him, "Uncle Duke"), joined a local writing club in his family's hometown of Litchfield, Minnesota. As he developed his writing skills, he would send us stories he had written. They were interesting stories, often about the family farm or family members. One day, he related to me the story of Karen Gorr whom he had met through his son and my cousin, David Hickler. The story he relayed to me was a jaw-dropping journey from disability to accomplishment.

I met Karen when I was visiting Litchfield. I was determined to help Uncle Duke and Karen tell Karen's story. Fortunately, I'd just launched my own publishing company, and had all the processes in place to take a good story and make it available to the world. I was motivated by meeting Karen and by two objectives. First, I felt Karen could inspire all of us to overcome obstacles, and second, I believe we have an inherent bias against the disabled and their abilities, and this needs to change.

We need to think about the disabled in terms of their opportunities to contribute, not their limitations.

The books I have written to date *look* like business books, because they talk about jobs and the workplace. But I am not only writing about business. I am writing about how to succeed, how to get jobs, how to listen, and how to get to "Next." What inspires me to write is the opportunity to help others get to Next, whatever that is for them. Karen's story reminded me that success lies in overcoming obstacles and how important "grit" is in the process of getting to Next. And while our obstacles may seem great, learning about someone like Karen and the obstacles she overcame should inspire all of us to realize just how small our own obstacles are.

We also all need to rethink our attitudes towards the disabled. A project manager at my media company, Dan, related to me a story from his personal life that echoes Karen's story and reflects cultural bias with respect to the disabled. In the early days of personal computers, Dan helped install a communication system for a young man named Chris who suffered from severe cerebral palsy. Chris spoke with great difficulty and had no use of his hands or feet. The communication system allowed Chris to "type" by making a clicking noise with his tongue to select letters from an on-screen keyboard.

Dan told me that, as he worked with Chris setting up the system, he mistook Chris' labored speech as a sign of limited intelligence. Dan would patronizingly ask, *"How are we today, Chris?"* Chris would struggle to say, "Goooood."

When the communication system was finally working, Dan said goodbye and wished Chris luck. About a week later, Dan unexpectedly received a computer-generated printout in the mail from Chris. It contained a prose poem based on the classic verse "No Man Is an Island" by John Donne. The gist of the poem was that Chris believed his new communication tool had rescued him from isolation on a deserted island.

At first, Dan was merely impressed that the technology worked so well and that Chris had written a literate, moving piece with it. But then, Dan had a sudden recollection of how he'd treated Chris as a person with limited intelligence for weeks and weeks during the setup process.

"My heart sank," Dan told me. "I could hardly believe that I mistook his slurred speech and facial contortions for mental disability, when all the time, there was a gifted and articulate writer trapped inside. I was ashamed." I know Dan, and he is a caring and sensitive person. But somewhere along the line, probably when he was very young, he'd developed biases about the disabled.

And so I challenge you to read Karen's story, a powerful tale of what can happen when an incredible person overcomes physical limitations and misguided and horrific government service through sheer willpower, determination, and a good dose of grit. *Life of Triumph* by Karen A. Gorr (as told to Duane Hickler) will inspire, entertain, and inspire you to "Get to NEXT," and change how you view and treat the next disabled person you encounter.

Cash Nickerson
Austin, TX
July 2016

Cash Nickerson and Karen.
Photo by Duane Hickler, used by permission.

DUANE'S STORY

This is a story of two miracles. Because of a little serendipity, I'm able to share it with you.

I have a son, David, who once was a custom harvester. He'd begin harvesting in the southern part of Texas and work his way north, clear to the Canadian Border. But he was forced to stop working because of a genetic lung disease called Alpha One.

While David was living in the small, midwestern town of Litchfield, Minnesota, he became friends with a woman who also lived in his building, Lincoln Apartments. Karen had cerebral palsy. Over time, as Karen and David became friends, she shared little bits and pieces of her life with him.

One day, while they were visiting together, Karen told him about the place where she'd spent much of her childhood — the State School and Home for the Feeble-Minded, in Redfield, South Dakota. As she talked, David realized he had harvested wheat around that very institution. David remembered asking the local farmers, "What is that place?" They had responded, "Oh, it's a place for crazy people."

As I heard about Karen's life, I felt inspired to write her story. I mentioned that to David. He replied, "I don't know if she would be willing to publicly share her story or not." I finally convinced him to ask her.

David did ask. Karen replied, "It's time my story is told."

Karen's story, I believe, will amaze you. She survived some extraordinary circumstances. Her spirit and her determination will capture your heart. But Karen did more than survive. She has made some significant contributions to society and to educating others. She has made this world a better place.

I feel honored to have the opportunity to help share her story with you.

My son's story is another miracle. He was told by many doctors in America that he had only a short time to live. Then he was treated in Mexico by Dr. Diaz. He is no longer on oxygen and has gone back to work. That's another story that needs to be told.

KAREN'S STORY

I spent ten-and-a-half years fighting two big battles: one with life and one with death.

I felt like a caged animal because of the bars on the windows.

Every door was always locked. A high fence surrounded the facility.

I was often beaten for minor things and sometimes for things I hadn't even done.

We had 15 minutes to eat, but the food wouldn't stay down.

Illness plagued me.

I couldn't walk, or I would have tried to run away.

This was life in the State School and Home for the Feeble- Minded.

My name is Karen.

A Life of Triumph is the true story of my family as I told it to my friend, Duane Hickler. As I talked, he typed my stories on his computer. We then worked together to edit them and put them in chronological order. Duane also did quite a bit of research on some topics covered in this book. I could not have created this book alone. Without Duane's help, this book would never have become a reality.

Hard Beginnings

I was born in 1937 in Monte Vista, Colorado. My brother, David, was two years older. When he was three, he fell out of our family's Model A Ford and struck his head on a cement curb. After that, he began to experience blackouts that got more frequent as the years went on. When I was three, I became seriously ill with what doctors believed was rickets, a disease caused by vitamin C deficiency. I went from being a cute, cuddly baby to a limp rag doll.

In the spring of 1940, our father passed away.

To support us, our mother, Mabel, worked two jobs as a waitress. But times were very tough. With two handicapped children, our mother found it hard to find and keep a babysitter. People in our small town were malicious and didn't understand how anyone could have two children who desperately needed medical help. They said, "There must be something wrong with their mother, too."

Our family should have had our father's Social Security checks, but they didn't arrive. Mother repeatedly checked with Social Security but could never get an answer. It turned out that mother's father-in-law, who was friends with the local postmaster, had been picking up the checks and cashing them. With the money, he built a cabin in the woods. Meanwhile, he'd told everyone he was saving the money for his two grandkids.

Mother decided to move us to South Dakota, where she had friends. Times were hard for most people, but for us, things went from bad to worse. Our mother developed a tumor on her back that had to be removed. Doctors gave her a 50-50 chance of surviving the surgery. This was the turning point that forced her to find someone, or someplace, that would care for us.

Seeking Solutions

Mother took us to the Mayo Clinic at Rochester, Minnesota, and to the Crippled Children's Home in Jamestown, North Dakota. We were examined and diagnosed at both places.

But both places turned us away. Why? One: We were fatherless. Two: We were poor. Three: There were two of us in the same family. People were generally unsympathetic. One doctor told mother she should do what the Japanese sometimes did with children like us — take us to a high cliff, push us over the side, and forget us. Mother told him where he could go!

Then, our mother learned of a place that would accept us both. To her, it seemed like a nice place with its highly polished marble floors and beautiful, well-tended lawns. This was the State School and Home for the Feeble Minded in Redfield, South Dakota.

David and Karen

LIFE IN A STATE INSTITUTION

Day One

When we arrived at the State School and Home for the Feeble Minded in Redfield, South Dakota, David and I were separated. David was taken away to the south building of the complex, and I was placed in the north building. My building housed people of all ages, from three-year-olds to senior citizens, and with all kinds of disabilities.

The very first day, the staff mixed up our slippers. I had David's and he had mine. Of course, I wanted my own slippers. I was three years old and very headstrong. The staff refused to make the switch. So I got mad. The staff tried to calm me down by bringing me a banana. I refused to calm down. Instead, I threw that banana across the beautiful marble floor and it smashed all over.

Why didn't the staff make things right? It would have been so easy. That was just the first of many things that, to this day, remain hard to understand. (I still have David's red slippers.)

Getting Around

With my cerebral palsy, I couldn't walk. To get around, I had to slide along the floor, pushing myself along with my arms, just like babies do before they learn to crawl. The marble floors of the institution were very well waxed, which made them very slippery. At least they kept them clean.

Never Enough to Eat

I was always hungry. At mealtimes, we had 15 minutes to eat everything on our plates. Because of my condition, I found it impossible to eat quickly. But the people in charge thought 15 minutes was plenty of time. No exceptions. I managed to get the food down, but it wouldn't stay down longer than 10 minutes.

I didn't like rutabagas. I would not eat them. Once, we were served rutabagas for the evening meal. I refused to eat them, so I went to bed hungry. The next morning at breakfast, the rutabagas appeared on my plate. They were back at lunch, and again at supper. By now I was really hungry, but I would not eat those rutabagas.

For the next two days, I got hungrier and hungrier. I wouldn't relent. Finally, the rutabagas began to get moldy and they were thrown out. It took two days of holding out, but my stubbornness finally won that battle.

But there was one downside. Staff began showing movies on Wednesday nights. Sometimes that was also rutabaga night. I loved movies. But I hated rutabagas more. So I missed a lot of movies, and I was sent to bed hungry.

Yes, I was always hungry. Maybe you remember those big jars of white paste. We used that paste for art work in school. Sometimes, to relieve my hunger pains, I'd even eat that paste. This helped a little, at least until I got caught. And when I did, I was slapped.

But I was resourceful. When the weather was nice, we got to spend time outside. There was a large weeping willow tree with branches that reached all the way to the ground. I loved this tree. I could crawl under the branches and hide in the hollow they made. In that hollow, the ground was moist. So I figured out that I could make mud pies. I ate those mud pies to keep the hunger away. I was always careful to have something with me that I could use to wipe off the mud. If anyone knew I'd been eating mud, I'd have been punished.

I had a friend who was a few years older than me and worked in the kitchen. She'd sometimes sneak food up to me and hide it in the big coat closet. Then, to make sure Mrs. B. didn't catch us, we'd sneak way into the back of the closet to eat it.

There was one food I especially liked: spiced peaches. We didn't have them often — only on holidays. But every time we had them, I'd always manage to hide some in my pockets and sneak them back to my room. I did it, even though the juice leaked out into my pockets. I was still sliding around on the floors to get around, but even so, I managed to share the peaches without getting caught. I was resourceful!

Morning and Night

My building of three floors housed females of all ages. I was on the first floor and slept in a large room full of beds. The beds were very close together. The lights came on at 5 a.m. sharp. Mrs. B. was the matron in charge of our building. She was like a drill sergeant. If you didn't get out of bed right away, she'd embarrass you. She'd come up to your bed and pull off not just your blankets, but your pajamas! I learned to listen for the click of the light switch and get up fast to make sure that didn't happen to me.

Every morning, we had to strip our beds. We had to remove all the bedding and even flip the mattresses over. Then we had to make our beds. I had to do this on my knees, and another girl helped me. There couldn't be a single wrinkle in the sheets or any of the other bedding, or Mrs. B. made us start the process all over again.

At night, before we got into bed, we had to remove the bedspread and the pillow. (We were never allowed to sleep with a pillow.) Then we had to fold everything up a certain way and put it on a large table at the back of the room. The bedspread and pillow could remain on the bed only during the day. If there was an inspection, everything had to look good.

Night held other problems. Sometimes I'd kick the covers off my bed. To stop me from doing this, Mrs. B. would fasten me to the bed by tying the covers under the bed. Sometimes, to get me in trouble, another girl would pour water on my covers to make it look like I'd wet the bed. There was nothing I could do. According to Mrs. B., bedwetting was an "unforgivable sin." So I was beaten. I was beaten often.

Remember that everyone from toddlers to senior citizens lived in my building. We were allowed to take one bath a week. We had to line up in the nude and wait our turn for the bath. In that line were people with all kinds of disabilities. Someone was always watching us. If we didn't get our elbows or knees clean, Mrs. B. went after them with a wire brush. I got around by dragging myself across the floor using my arms, so I was usually a target for the wire brush.

Early School Days

Most of us children went to "school" in the institution five days a week. I didn't have to crawl to school. Instead, I went in a wheelchair. School provided very little formal education. We learned music, arts and crafts, and had a gym class. Those who could read were given books.

I was one of the lucky ones. A kind, motherly woman named Dorothy Maskers was a patient in my ward. She was paralyzed from her shoulders, down. She taught me and other children how to read, print, and play Parcheesi. Dorothy took me under her wing. She was very special.

Learning to Protect Myself

I constantly had to fight illnesses that plagued my already weak body. Not being able to keep food down didn't help. But my personality helped me survive. I was different than most of the other children. Stubborn and bullheaded, I had a strong will to live. But my bullheadedness also got me into trouble. I fought anyone or anything that stood in my way.

For example, I didn't often get to see my brother, David. The rule was that we could see each other once every six months and when our mother came for her yearly visits. I wasn't even allowed to acknowledge David when we passed in the hallways. But I didn't care. He was my brother. I'd say, "Hi, David," and he'd reply, "Hi, Sissy." That always earned me a slap across the face.

I did learn how to protect myself after a fashion. I protected my face by ducking my head into my right elbow. This became so ingrained that even years later, when I lived at home, if someone started walking towards me, I'd duck like that without even realizing it.

I got paddled a lot. I figured out how to protect myself from that, too. I'd get my legs up and swing them over and around my neck, then roll over so my butt stuck up. So when people swung at my face, they got my butt instead. Later, when I moved home, I'd show my cousins how I did this. I could even chew on my toenails in this position. It grossed them out, but they laughed with me.

The worst punishment didn't have to do with getting beaten or slapped. My friend, Dorothy, who taught me how to read, couldn't use any part of her body except her hands. She couldn't even put on her own shoes and socks. I loved Dorothy, and she let me put her shoes and socks on for her. It made me feel good, and I loved being able to help Dorothy. One day — I don't remember what I'd done — but it must have been really bad because my punishment felt worse than a beating. Dorothy wouldn't let me help her with her shoes and socks. Dorothy, herself, delivered this punishment, which made it hurt all the more.

My aggressive disposition got me into other kinds of trouble. The doctors sometimes used me as a guinea pig. They gave me shock treatments that almost killed me. They tried phenobarbital on me. Once, I was given nine of these, and I got seriously ill.

Doing Chores: Learning to Adapt

We all had to wash our socks and underwear in the sink at night because we only had two pairs of each. You might wonder how I did this. I grabbed hold of the sink and pulled myself up, and a friend would help me. The way I got around, crawling and sliding along the floor, put plenty of holes in my socks. Kind Dorothy taught me how to darn them. I still have the darning bulb she gave me when I was five years old.

As soon as the staff thought we were able to help, they assigned each one of us another patient who needed extra care and help. I was assigned to help another little girl. She was younger than I was and had Down Syndrome. I helped her dress and wash her hands and face, and made sure she brushed her teeth.

When I was five, I was asked to help the girl whose bed was next to mine. This girl had problems with seizures. I'd tell her not to get up until she had her medicine. But often she wouldn't listen. Then she'd have a seizure and fall to the floor. This happened many times. But as long as the staff could get the medicine to her while she was still in bed, this girl wouldn't have a problem.

I did learn how to dust. In fact, I was known for doing it well. That was good because the place had lots of furniture. But Mrs. B. had eyes like a hawk. If I missed even one tiny spot, I was in for a slap.

Punishments Get Worse

The institution was a dog-eat-dog world. I did have some friends, and most of the ward matrons considered me a pet or favorite. All except Mrs. B. I will never forget Mrs. B. She was the meanest person I knew on the institution staff. When I was nine, someone accused me of something I didn't do. Nevertheless, Mrs. B. beat me from my shoulders clear down to my buttocks. My back was a mess of open wounds. They hurt so much I couldn't lie on my back that night. All night, I prayed to God that my mother would visit the next day. I knew it wasn't time for her yearly visit, but I prayed anyway. My prayers were answered!

The next morning, David and I met our mother at the Main Office Building. I told mom to look at my back. Mom screamed, "Who did this to you?"

We went to see the administrator, Dr. C., and he asked me what had happened and who had done this to me. I told him the story. Right then, he called Mrs. B. on the phone and asked her how everything was in her building. Of course, she said everything was going just great. But then he told her why he was calling and who was in his office with him. Mrs. B. said I'd fallen down some stairs. I screamed into the phone, "That's not true! You did this to me for something I did not do!"

Mrs. B. never beat me again, but still found ways to show her mean personality. When I was 10, Mrs. B. was upset with me about something. As a punishment, she told me to kneel with my arms folded behind my back.

Other patients were punished this way, but it was very hard for me to hold this position. As soon as I'd start to fall over, Mrs. B. would pull me up and make me kneel again. She did this time and time again, and my knees bled. Finally, Mrs. B. gave up.

My Brother, David: Love and Loss

David's temperament was not like mine. He was mistreated by staff, but didn't respond the way I did. He was older, but he was also more mature.

The institution had a large garden, and as David got older, he worked in that garden. On the way to the garden, David had to pass my building. I'd watch for him so we could meet on his way back. Sometimes, he'd sneak fresh veggies to me. I'd hide them, then enjoy them in private.

We never got to spend Christmas Day together with our mom. But the institution did have an annual Christmas program, and that was one time I could be with my brother. All the patients got a chance to perform. David and I sang a duet of "Away in a Manger." Even today, when I remember that time, my eyes fill with tears.

The blackouts David suffered from the car accident continued. Every time he had one, he fell face down. When he was 13, he developed pneumonia. He was taken to the hospital. But I wasn't allowed to visit him.

On a cold February day, a woman, who was also a patient, came to the school with a wheelchair to take me to the Main Office Building. My first thought was, *maybe my mom is here.* Halfway to the office, the woman stopped to put on her scarf. Right at that moment, something — a quiet voice — told me David had died. I started to cry.

The woman begged me to stop crying. She'd been instructed not to tell me about David. I assured her and the Office Matron that no one had told me about David. I'd just gotten a message in my head, almost like a premonition. They told me that in the hospital, David had had one of his blackouts and had passed away.

The weather was stormy. A blizzard kept mom from getting to Redfield. The staff put David's body on a train and sent him to mom in Pierre, South Dakota. I couldn't attend the funeral. This was terribly upsetting. I never got to say goodbye to my brother.

My Determination Grows

I was a fighter. I had to do something about Mrs. B.'s continued punishments. I wanted to talk to Dr. C. Two days later, I asked a girlfriend, who was also a patient in my building, to help. We discovered Mrs. B. had forgotten to lock the outside door. The door was very heavy and too hard for me to open. So my friend opened it for me. She looked around to make sure no one was in sight, then gave me the signal to crawl through. I made it.

Just outside my building was a large landscaped area with a tall, prickly hedge next to a paved road. I crawled across the grass to reach the hedge. But there were no openings in the hedge, and it was too thick to get through. I had to get past it to reach Dr. C. in the Administration Building.

This was a time when my cerebral palsy actually helped me. Some people with cerebral palsy become very stiff and unable to move. But I was fortunate. I was as flexible as a rag doll. So I leaned up against the hedge, did a back flip, went over the hedge, and landed on the paved road.

The Administration Building was across the street and two or three blocks away. It was a long crawl, but I made it.

My next challenge was getting up the long flight of cement steps that led into the building. Here's what I did. I sat on the bottom step, grabbed the hand rail, then pulled and dragged myself up to the next step. I did this over and over, one step at a time. I had to stop several times to rest, but I finally reached the top.

Then I was confronted by a big, heavy door. I couldn't open it, so I pounded on it. A secretary inside heard the pounding but couldn't see me. Finally, she opened the door to see what was going on and found me lying there, all dirty and bleeding. She said, "What happened?" I told her, "I want to speak to Dr. C." So she cleaned me up and took me to his office.

I told Dr. C. about the punishments. He said, "I will take you home." He picked me up and carried me to his car. I thought to myself, "Wow, I'm going with the big boss."

He drove over to my building and carried me in. When Mrs. B. saw us, she turned white. Dr. C. asked, "What happened to Karen?" Mrs. B. replied, "She must have fallen down." She hadn't even missed me. Dr. C. said, "I think you know what happened." Then he proceeded to give her a tongue lashing.

David's slippers

GOODBYE TO THE INSTITUTION

An Important Summer

I knew I wouldn't survive in that institution. I would have tried to escape, but I couldn't walk. Besides, I knew I'd never be able to make it past the high wall that surrounded the facility. I'd heard that if you made it across the state border, you were free. Two older girls did escape. They made it across the border and were never caught.

When I was 13, in 1950, I begged mom to take me out of that prison. I was allowed to go home for the summer. Mom told me that if I learned to walk during the few months I had at home, maybe I could stay home for good.

That was an important summer. I had a good doctor who told me that I could do anything I wanted if I made up my mind to do it.

I Learn to Walk

Walking! I made that my goal. The same attitude that kept getting me into trouble at the institution was now my ally. At home, I could take my time eating. I could eat as much as I wanted. I had never experienced that. I started to gain weight. I got stronger. I kept after my goal, trying over and over again. And you know what? I did learn to walk, in my own way. I felt so encouraged. I began to feel I could do anything — that the whole world was at my fingertips.

I Go to School

Things began to get better. That fall, I was allowed to enter country school. I was 13 and in the third grade. My school was 17 miles west of Pierre, South Dakota. But there was a new hurdle. To get to the school, my teacher had to drive past our house. So my mom arranged for her to pick me up. But she wouldn't let the teacher drive down our driveway to our house. Instead, I had to walk the quarter mile to meet her at the highway. Yes, I was walking by then, but it was still a struggle.

The first day, I walked to the highway, which was a real challenge. Our driveway went down a hill, so when I tried to walk, I'd fall down, get up, try to walk some more, and fall down again. By the time I made it down the hill, my hands and knees were scraped and my knees were bleeding. The very next day, my teacher brought along a bucket of water, a washcloth, and some bandages so I could wash off the blood and bandage my knees. What a kind and wonderful person she was. And she was also an excellent teacher. Eventually, I got so much better at walking that I could make it down the driveway without falling. I attended that school for two years.

Christmas at Home

Christmas with my family was such a contrast to Christmas at the institution! Mom and I celebrated with seven cousins and other relatives. Among my gifts were a doll and a game of Parcheesi. My cousins were very good to me, but the best was being with mom. It was a great Christmas.

A NEW SCHOOL
IN SIOUX FALLS

In 1952, I moved to Sioux Falls, and for two years lived in the brand new Crippled Children's Hospital and School. Dr. Morrison became the facility's director in 1951, supervised the completion of the building, and opened it on March 9, 1952. I was one of its first residents.

Dr. Morrison was very bald. So we kids took the tune to "On Top of Old Smokey" and changed the words around to fit Dr. Morrison:

> "On top of old baldy, all covered with fuzz,
> He lost all his hair cause he washed it with DUZZ."

We thought it was pretty funny. (We were careful to never sing it when he was nearby.)

To tell you the truth, I wasn't a very good student. When I was younger, I was always given IQ tests. I'd taken them so many times, I'd memorized them. When I was in the seventh grade, I began to think that if I gave the wrong answers on purpose, I'd look smart. But over time, I wised up. I worked at it and became a really good student.

I had a couple of adventures while attending school in Sioux Falls. One summer, an organization chose me to go to summer camp at Lake Kempeska. They bought me a raincoat and everything I needed for camping, and gave me three dollars for spending money.

The following summer, the Shriners Association chose me as the Poster Child of South Dakota. They gave me money to buy a nice dress that I wore in the Shriners Parade in Sioux Falls.

In junior high, I joined a student nursing club. The leaders decided they wanted to go visit the institution where I'd been locked up for ten years. But they didn't know I'd lived there. I wrote to the Administrator to tell him I was coming with the group, but I didn't want to do the tour. All I wanted to do was visit my old friend Dorothy Maskers, who'd been so kind to me and had taught me to read. The Administrator agreed to that. Neither he nor I ever told the group that I'd once lived there.

When I was 15, Grandma Huffman, who was divorced from Grandpa Huffman, took me to meet my grandfather. Remember, he was the one who took the Social Security checks our mom needed so desperately when we were little. When I walked in to meet him, he said, "You must be Karen." I said I was. Then grandpa stepped back, took a good look at me, and seemed shocked I was able to walk. He said one word: "Wow." He was nice to me and gave me a hug.

When I was in high school, he wrote me a letter. I think he was trying to atone for his sins. I have that letter to this day. I don't remember ever seeing any family pictures.

Another interesting thing happened in Sioux Falls. I met the school dietitian, June Foss, who had a daughter with cerebral palsy. June and her husband, Joe, told me that if I went to church with them on Sundays, they'd buy me lunch. So I did. I went to church with them regularly and got to know the family very well. We became great friends. Joe later became the governor of South Dakota.

After living in Sioux Falls for a couple of years, in 1954, I moved back to Pierre, South Dakota, to live with mom and finish junior high school. Dr. Morrison told my mom, "Karen will never make it through high school, but let her try it."

HIGH SCHOOL AND THE GOVERNOR'S MANSION

After Joe Foss became Governor of South Dakota, I was asked to move into the Governor's Mansion and stayed there for my sophomore through senior years of high school. I had a lot of responsibility in their home. My job was to tutor their daughter, Cheryl, who was two years younger than me and who had cerebral palsy. She wore metal braces from her feet all the way up to her hips and used crutches that went all the way to her elbows. I also did some cleaning and helped around the house. There were two other children, Frank and Mary Jo, and Governor Foss's mother also lived with them. I always called Joe "Governor Joe," and he called me "girlie."

The Governor had a great sense of humor and was a joy to be around. When we ate a meal together, Governor Foss always dished up the food. When he was filling my plate, I'd always say, "Not too much, please," but he would laugh and fill it up.

We had many interesting times together. A surprising thing happened when the Foss's son, Frank, was three. One night, the Governor and his wife, June, were gone on some official business. I was in the house with the three children and Joe's mother. Suddenly, in the middle of the night, something woke me with a start. Someone was pounding on the front door. I raced to the door and unlocked it. There stood a cop holding little Frank. Apparently, he had been sleepwalking. He managed to open the front door and wander around the grounds. There was a pool on the grounds! I was terrified.

I picked him up, took him to his bed, and spent the night sleeping on the floor right next to his bed. The next day, a workman came and put a higher latch on the door. I never got in trouble over it.

Home with the Fosses

There were some amusing times. One day, the Italian Ambassador was coming to meet with Governor Foss. June asked me to make some very dainty cookies — three triple-sized batches. The cookies were supposed to be no bigger than a quarter. But the first batch came out huge! They were the size of a pancake or a small plate.

We had to get rid of those. So the three kids and I, and Joe's mom, ate some of them. The maintenance man also pitched in and offered to give the rest to the horses.

Luckily, the other batches turned out the way they were supposed to, and June never found out about the first batch, as she was gone for a few days. But I bet she would have had a good laugh about it.

Life in that house was full of adventures. One time, Governor Joe and June were both gone, and I was taking care of the kids. It was suppertime. I'd made a full meal, including mashed potatoes. Cheryl, Mary Jo, Frank, and I were eating in the kitchen, and Joe's mom was eating in Joe's office, which she liked to do when he was gone. Mary Jo, who was probably in about the third grade, began throwing spoonfuls of mashed potatoes at Cheryl. I told her to stop or she would have to go to her room. Mary Jo crawled under the table. Now, remember that Cheryl had metal braces on her legs. Under the table were the chair legs and Cheryl's legs with their braces. Mary Jo got tangled up around the chair leg and Cheryl's braces. It took me quite a while to get her out.

Mary Jo had been naughty, so I decided to take her upstairs to her room. I told Cheryl and Frank to wait while I did that. But as Mary Jo and I reached the top of the stairs, we both realized that Cheryl was right behind us. With her braces and crutches, it was extremely unusual for Cheryl to move that fast. But she was nosy and wanted to see what was going to happen to Mary Jo. When we saw how close Cheryl was, we all burst out laughing. Mary Jo helped me clean up the mess in the kitchen, then we all finished our supper. No one got punished. Instead, we laughed.

The fact is, I'd always worried how I'd be able to get Cheryl out in a hurry if there was ever a fire when I was alone with the kids. This proved Cheryl could move fast if she really had to.

Once, I was even in a style show! June Foss had organized a tea party in the Governor's Mansion to raise money for cerebral palsy. Many celebrities had sent in their hats to be auctioned off. Even Pat Nixon, Vice President Nixon's wife, sent her hat. I was dressed really nicely for the occasion, thanks to June. I got to wear Pat Nixon's hat! I felt like a queen for the day. A picture of me wearing the hat even appeared in the Pierre *Capital Journal* newspaper!

I do have one regret about the Fosses. Years later, I went to visit them. Governor Foss asked if I'd like to go to the Orange Bowl with him. June did not want to go and encouraged me to attend. "It will be a great experience for you," she said. At first, I said, "Oh, I can't get off from work." Joe said, "I'll call them and take care of that." I came back with, "But I don't have nice enough clothes." And Joe said, "We'll take you shopping and buy you clothes." And I said, "But I won't know any of the women." As I look back, I regret I didn't go. I had a great relationship with the Foss family. I really was part of the family.

Back to the Institution

While I lived with the Fosses, I asked Governor Joe if he'd make a surprise visit to what was now called the Redfield State Hospital and School, where I'd spent 10 years of my life. I said it was very important that they let him inspect a certain building that had a basement. Joe agreed to do it.

When Joe arrived at the institution, the gate guard recognized him. He had no choice but to let him in. As Joe completed the tour, he asked to see the building I'd told him about. At first, the tour guide told him it was an unimportant building, but Governor Joe demanded to see it.

When they reached the building, again the tour guide tried to keep Governor Joe from going in. They couldn't keep him out. Joe opened the door and found himself in a basement where human beings, many with no clothing, were lying in their own waste. The scene was so horrific that the Governor became ill. Once he was out of the building, he began vomiting.

Governor Joe was a decorated soldier. He'd earned a Medal of Honor. He'd seen the worst that war could deliver. Yet the scene he had just witnessed in Redfield, South Dakota, made him sick. Thus began the work of Governor Foss and his wife, June, to make changes in the conditions of all the state hospitals like the one at

Redfield. They worked behind the scenes. Changes were hard to come by, so change did not happen over night. June was a strong Republican and not afraid to speak up about what she thought should be done.

When I was in high school, Dr. Morrison brought a bus load of his students from Sioux Falls to visit. He was one of the professional people who told me I'd never be able to graduate from high school. During that visit, he met with me and said I'd fooled him. He was very proud of me. He said, "Keep up the good work."

In 1958, I graduated from high school. I was 21 years old.

I GO TO COLLEGE

In September, 1958, I began my studies at Northern State College in Aberdeen, South Dakota. I had help from scholarships and State grants, but I had to maintain a B average to keep them. To pay for my room and board, I also worked as a dorm counselor.

My dream was to be a teacher. My freshman-year advisor told me I was doing an excellent job in school, and I'd make a wonderful teacher. I was so excited to be on my way to fulfilling my dream! My sophomore year, I applied for a student teaching class and met with my advisor — the same one I'd had freshman year. This year, she told me I didn't have a chance at making it as a teacher. I was so surprised. I asked what had changed her mind. She said I didn't walk well enough or talk plain enough.

I was never one to take no for an answer. So I went to talk to the Dean of the college. He told me to go to physical therapy, and also see a speech therapist. How on earth was I going to pay for that?

My speech therapist had only one arm, but rode motorcycles. He'd probably had some adversity in his life. Well, he told me never to be late for an appointment. I made up my mind to always be early. He accepted that as payment for my speech lessons. My physical therapist had a young child. To pay for my speech lessons, I did babysitting.

Then, the Dean of the college arranged a meeting with me and some of my former professors. They would give their opinion as to my teaching future.

Of course, I was frightened. We spent some intense time together. They asked questions. I answered. Then they asked me to wait outside the door while they talked some things over and made their decision.

While I waited, with my boyfriend, Jim, at my side, I thought, *What am I going to do if they say I can't continue studying to be a teacher? I don't want to go back and live with my mother. Maybe I can go back and live with the Foss family and work for them.*

At last, they called me in to hear their decision. The Dean said, "Karen, you did wonderfully in here. Go finish your degree and teach." I was so happy!

The Dean gave me written permission for my student teaching class. Among my advisors for my student teaching were those who had told me I'd never make it. Well, I showed them. I finished my course with a B+, and went on to get my Bachelor of Science degree in Special Education.

FIRST LOVE

I had started dating a guy in the school cafeteria. At first, Jim and I would just get together in the cafeteria or at the library. One day, he asked whether I was going home that weekend. I told him no, but I lied. He later asked me if I'd really meant to go home, and I admitted I'd thought about it. This was the start of a great friendship.

Jim realized how badly I wanted to learn how to drive, so he agreed to teach me to drive his stick shift. I was doing very well, but I had one major problem. I had trouble staying on the right side of the road. Jim would scold me and warn me. Finally, his patience wore thin. He got frustrated and yelled, "Honey, will you please stay on the right side of the road!" After that, I managed to stay on the right side of the road.

We got engaged. Jim gave me a ring, and we made wedding plans. Jim was a couple years ahead of me and graduated from Northern State in December. He decided to enter the National Guard to complete his service to his country. He was doing basic training in

Ford Ord, California, and had come home on leave. On his way back to California, Jim was involved in a traffic accident. He was riding in a double-decker Greyhound bus. At Emigrant Gap in California, the bus collided with a California State Highway pickup truck that was making a left-hand turn. The bus broadsided the truck and the results were devastating. The pickup truck driver was killed. The bus went off the road, rolled down an embankment, then crashed against a clump of trees. Jim was killed, too. Another soldier and a woman were also killed. All three were riding in the upper deck. The bus driver was not injured. This happened just three months before our wedding date.

I didn't know how I was going to get through this. Just like all young lovers, we were excited about our wedding. We were thinking of having a family. Now those dreams were shattered. This loss seemed unbearable. I became depressed. I struggled to make sense of it; I struggled against the depression. I'd overcome a lot of challenges in my life, and this was another hurdle. I called on my survival skills, and gradually, over time, I began to pull myself together.

The pain lasted, though. Several years later, I was visiting relatives in California. A cousin and I were driving along Highway 40, and suddenly there stood the sign for Emigrant Gap. This was the spot where Jim had died. I was able to look down the embankment and was shocked to see how steep it was. This was a very emotional time for me. All kinds of memories came back — thoughts of what our lives together would have been, and the magnitude of our loss. I wept.

TEACHING INTERNSHIPS

My Old "Home"

Imagine the irony of it. I had an internship teaching the physically handicapped at the Sioux Falls Crippled Children's Hospital and School, the very place I'd spent those tough years as a student some 10 years earlier. Many of the same nurses, teachers, and therapists were still employed there. But now, I was their equal. Some of them were extremely unfair and overly critical of my performance, but I proved to them that I could be a good teacher.

While I had that internship, I lived with a young family I'd met at the school 10 years earlier. Mr. and Mrs. H. had two adorable children and lived in a very nice house just six blocks from the school. I could easily walk to school. The H. family treated me as one of their own. I had my own living quarters in the basement, which I paid for by cleaning, cooking, and babysitting.

Mr. and Mrs. H. were friends of Dr. Morrison and were involved in founding and starting the Crippled Children's Hospital and School, where Mrs. H. was a certified teacher. Mr. and Mrs. H. were completely supportive of me and encouraged me to accomplish my goal of becoming a teacher.

University of Iowa

The next summer, I enrolled as a student at the University of Iowa. I drove by myself from Pierre, South Dakota to Iowa City. It's interesting that the same Dr. Morrison, who had told my mother I'd never graduate from high school, had gotten his degree from the university I now attended with a full scholarship!

Mom had always had a hard time encouraging me and often told me I could have done better. So imagine how huge it was for me when she told me she was proud of me for getting that scholarship.

I arrived at my dorm and began moving in my things. It was a wonderful room and even had a phone. As I was getting settled in, there was a knock at the door. In stepped a beautiful girl who said, "Hi, my name is Connie, and I'm your roommate."

There was one surprise. Connie was black. I'd never known a black person. And I have to say, the thing that went through my mind was, *I don't think I'm prejudiced. I guess now I will find out.*

Making Friends

A week after we met, Connie asked me, "Do you have a problem having a black person as your roommate?" I assured her that I did not. Connie then told me that every other white person had rejected her as a roommate. Connie was a great roommate, and we became very good friends.

Over the 4th of July, Connie invited me to go home with her to Des Moines, Iowa. This was another new experience for me. Connie's parents did not have a fancy home, but it was very clean, and they and Connie's younger sister treated me like I was family. In the mornings, we woke up to the smell of eggs, coffee, bacon, and pancakes that her father was making. The family made maple syrup from their own trees.

When I rode in the car with Connie's family, people stared. Here was this blonde, white girl in a carload of black people. Connie's sister noticed that white people were staring at us. She said, "I think those white folks think we must have kidnapped you." Know what I did? As we drove along, I just smiled and waved to them.

Connie and I had something in common. It was easy enough to see that I had a disability. I walked with a slight limp and sometimes had problems speaking clearly. But Connie also faced a challenge. That challenge was her color. Some of her professors didn't give her the grades she deserved because she was black. When she went to the Dean and showed him her grades, he told her there was nothing he could do about it. It took her three years longer to graduate. Connie was very intelligent, but she also had to overcome the prejudice of what I called her "color disability." Connie went on to become a medical doctor, and her sister became an attorney.

Also in my dorm lived 25 nuns, just down the hall from me. On the floor below were 50 people from Spain who didn't speak English, but had interpreters. Across the hall from Connie and me was a girl from Massachusetts, who had ridden the train from Boston to Iowa City, accompanied by three very large, live turtles. This girl had a great Boston accent and was a lot of fun. One day, a turtle escaped, but no one was ever able to find it. Someone probably had turtle soup.

One guy from Nigeria who spoke just a little English asked me to go with him to a club. I wasn't sure what kind of club it was, but he seemed like such a nice guy. I decided to go. It turned out great. The club was international, with people from all over the world. This was another great experience.

The time I spent in Iowa was definitely the highlight of my life to this point. For my internship, I taught physically handicapped children from 8 a.m. to noon, Monday through Friday. Then I helped an eight-year-old boy improve his ability to read and to reach his required level. I was exposed to so many new things, from living with and becoming friends with someone of another race to meeting people from all over the world. All of this was part of a great education, and a far cry from living in the State School and Home for the Feeble-Minded in Redfield, South Dakota.

JOB TIME

It was inevitable. One day, I would have to have my first job interview. The fateful day arrived. I'd spent many hours preparing for this. I had to look neat, clean, and well-dressed — the standard for every working person. My biggest concern was my speech. As the time for my interview grew closer, these words kept going through my mind: Remember to talk slowly and enunciate each word clearly.

Mr. Nerd arrived. Dr. Morrison introduced me, then left us alone in a large conference room. I answered several questions and gradually began to feel very confident and at ease with Mr. Nerd. It sounded like I was going to get the job of teaching about 10 Sioux Indian children in a one-room country school house.

I anticipated the offer and prematurely asked for a couple of days to think it over. Mr. Nerd then dropped the bomb. He said to me, "Miss Huffman, would you please walk around the room for me?" I was stunned.

I think I just sat there for a minute. He repeated his request. I replied, "I can hop like a bunny, too! Would you like to see me?" End of interview. End of Mr. Nerd. The name fit.

The next interviewer was much kinder and more interested in my qualifications and abilities than my disabilities. I was hired to set up a Special Education Classroom in Parkston, South Dakota, and teach five children, ages six through 10, with mental special needs and learning disabilities. I taught there for two years. After that, drawing on all the skills I'd learned in Iowa City the summer before, I set up a classroom in Sioux City, Iowa, where for two years I taught 10 physically handicapped children.

Living in a Mortuary

In Sioux City, I rented an apartment with a roommate. Our apartment was over a mortuary owned by a guy we called by his initials: JR. I had a bad habit of forgetting my keys, especially at night. I'd have to call JR to let me in. Finally, he told me about a back door I could use that was never locked. The entrance through the back led into the room where JR kept the bodies and did the embalming work. He warned me to always be sure to go back and turn off the light, and carry a flashlight when I came in that way.

One night, I realized I'd forgotten my key and my flashlight. But I figured that if anyone was back there, they were dead so they couldn't hurt me. As I made my way back, I bumped into something. It turned out to be a toe with a tag on it, sticking out from a body. You bet I screamed. I never, ever again forgot my keys or my flashlight.

Sometimes, in the evening, my roommate and I would cross the bridge from Sioux City, Iowa into Sioux City, Nebraska. There, we met two guys in a bar and had fun visiting with them. They wanted to know where we lived, but we weren't ready to share that. This friendship continued for some time. Eventually, we told them we lived in an apartment above a funeral home. We invited them to come visit. The guys thought about it, then agreed to come.

I asked JR if we could show our friends around and play a little trick on them. JR agreed to it and showed us a casket we could use. The evening the guys were coming, I fixed up my roommate with white makeup, a black wig, and a black gown.

Well, the guys arrived and asked where my friend was. I told them she'd gone on a short errand. I invited them in, then acting like a salesperson, I began showing them the caskets. As we looked at one, I said, "This one is for a man," and I proceeded to show them why. Then we approached another one and I explained, "This is a casket for a woman." I opened it slowly and up sat my friend. One guy ran, and the other wet his pants. They never came back. JR was watching from his office. We all had a great laugh!

When I went back to Northern State to complete my studies for my degree, an older English professor told me to write a short dissertation on an unusual subject. I wrote a paper titled, "Preparation for the Internment of the Deceased," which I'd learned all about from JR. When I turned in my paper, the professor took one look at the first page and turned white. He quickly marked it with an A, handed it back, and said, "Go, goodbye, we're done."

Teaching in Gaylord

Later, I was hired as a special education teacher in Gaylord, Minnesota. I'd been there three or four months and had become friends with some other single teachers who asked me to join their bowling team. In college, I'd been required to take a sport and took bowling. When I met with the bowling instructor, he told me to arrive early to sign up. When the class met, he asked for a volunteer to act as secretary and keep track of all the paperwork. I raised my hand. He told me if I did that, I'd be assured of an A, no matter how badly I bowled.

Everyone else had told me I'd never get a passing grade because of my handicap. I started out with pretty low scores, but by the end of the class, I could maintain a 125 average. That wasn't a great score. But, considering I hadn't started walking until I was 13, I thought it was pretty good.

Dale

None of us teachers wanted to bowl in Gaylord, so we drove the 26 miles to St. Peter. We took turns driving. We were all average bowlers, but we had lots of fun on our "girls nights out." After bowling, we liked to stop for some fast food. Sometimes, we'd go to Winthrop for a beer or two. We always bowled early, so it was early when we got back to Gaylord.

Back then, it was frowned upon for single women teachers to go into Gaylord's Liquor Store. So, if we wanted anything, we drove to Winthrop. After I'd stopped a few times at the Winthrop Liquor store, one of the bartenders called me for a date. Dale was very nice, polite, and sort of cute. He was nearly bald and short, and on the chubby side. For some time, I was convinced he was married with kids, or had been married with kids. I was so wrong.

About a year later, Dale and I began to date. Sometimes, I invited him and other friends to my house for supper. Eventually, Dale and I married.

Dale's Family

Dale's family background was quite unique. His parents, their siblings, grandparents, and some cousins immigrated to America from the Black Forest area of Germany. His grandparents were not very old as their oldest children were in their early teens. They were all transported to Nebraska where most of them worked for sugar beet farmers for their food, a place to live, and a small wage.

Over time, most of them, all related, moved from farm to farm to find bigger crops for better living conditions and more money. Dale's family members finally settled in Minnesota, in the towns of Gibbon, Winthrop, and Gaylord. Dale's mom and dad had married, raised five children, and moved to Winthrop before we met. They had learned to speak and write in English from going to school and church, but all of them spoke fluent German when at home with relatives. Dale's brother and 3 sisters, plus 17 nieces and nephews, spoke German when they were together. But not Dale. "Why?" I asked. "Because we live in America where most people speak English and this is our language," he replied. One stubborn German, huh?

All of Dale's relatives who had come to America were quite poor. They had spent many hours of hard labor working in those sugar beet fields, crawling on their hands and knees, digging up the beets, row after row, from dawn to dusk. Day after day, and year after year.

The children also worked at an early age as much as they were able. Dale's mom, at times, pulled him behind her in a basket when his sister and brother were needed in the field. His oldest sister would take him back to the home after a few hours to do some housework to help his mom. Everyone worked together. Come Sunday, everyone went to Church and prayed together.

To my best knowledge and memory, this is an accurate account of Dale's parent's life after they arrived in America, and became citizens.

Meeting Dale's family was a pleasant surprise as they all welcomed me with open arms, especially "Ma," his mom. All of the family called her Ma—even grandchildren, nieces, nephews, and in-laws. So I learned to call her Ma. Sadly, I never got to meet his Pa, or his older brother, as they had both died 1 ½ years earlier. By this time the three sisters and one brother had married and started families. Ma had 17 grandchildren who all understood and spoke German. Dale had come home from Korea, where he had fought on the front lines, and was luckier that a lot of his comrades. He rarely talked about Korea, just as I seldom talked about Redfield.

After we married, we lived in Winthrop. I felt a strong attraction to Ma from the first time we met. We became good friends. Sundays we'd go to church together, then usually to her house for a big dinner. I learned to eat and cook German foods, which Dale had grown up eating;

later our daughter grew up eating them. We would often take Ma out for buffet suppers which we really enjoyed. We took her to visit her three daughters, her son's wife and seven children, and for many years we all went to her oldest daughter's for deer hunting, which we all enjoyed.

Ma was a very special person to me! I truly don't think there are any people like her in the world. She was one of a kind and I still miss her. I also miss Dale, but he and I had a different special bond. Our daughter and Ma had a beautifully close relationship that doesn't exist between young and old very often any more. Those two, with a very big difference in age, were linked like soul mates of the same age, and thoroughly enjoyed being together. They were both very lucky to have had so much time together as we lived so close to her-we were all very lucky to have known Ma, until we meet again, all of you will live in my heart.

Karen and her husband Dale

*Karen and Dale with daugher Katie
at her graduation from High School*

THE ULTIMATE GIFT

I became pregnant. But again, with cerebral palsy, nothing was straightforward. I was five feet, one-and-a-half inches tall. Over the years, doctors had told me to keep my weight between 95 and 100 pounds. Pregnant, I weighed 117.7. I'd gained only 17 pounds, but that was too much weight for me. Because of my problem with balance, I'd begun to fall forward two or three times a day.

Also, I was "top heavy." The baby hadn't moved down into the birth canal and often kicked me in my ribs. Because of this, I couldn't stand, sit, or lie down comfortably for very long. My doctor's main concern was the risk to me and my baby if I had a natural birth. At four or five months, I had false labor pains. These, too, were scary, but thankfully, they lasted only two or three weeks.

Meanwhile, I kept busy, cleaning, cooking, and baking, and substituting at school when I was needed. I spent time getting to know my in-laws and their family members, going shopping, and going out for lunch. Most importantly, I was happy.

On April 17, 1969, at 7 p.m., I was admitted to the Gaylord, Minnesota hospital. A good friend came with me because Dale was working at his night job. He promised to come early the next morning. I was extremely worried about the next day because my doctor was in Rochester, Minnesota with his wife who had had heart surgery early that morning. He told the hospital that he'd be with me, along with a specialist, in the morning.

On the 18th, Dale got to the hospital at 6:30 a.m., and the doctor and the specialist were there by 8:00 a.m. I was very happy to see everyone, especially my doctor. He and I had spent many hours discussing all the pros and cons of my pregnancy and learning from each other. We had become good friends.

My doctor and the hospital team asked lots of questions and did some tests. They decided that because of my cerebral palsy and the balance problems it caused, it was less risky to do a C-section that day than to wait two months for a natural birth.

It was time. My doctor assured me, "We will take good care of you and your baby. Everything will be okay." Tears ran down my face and I managed to say, "God bless us all." My husband sat on my bed and restrained me as he held back his own tears. Soon, we would know whether our baby was a healthy, "normal" child or, as I had been called at Redfield, a "freak of nature."

In the OR, I was asked to count to 100. I took a deep breath and softly said, "God, please bless this child." And I was out.

When I woke up in my room, my husband was right there. He said, "She's perfect!" My prayers were answered — God had given us the Ultimate Gift. Here was yet another accomplishment the so-called experts had told me I should never consider.

My doctor came to see me. He said, "Karen, she's very tiny. She has trouble keeping her body temperature stable, so she'll be in the incubator for a couple days. Not to worry — she is, and will be, fine."

Dale's mom and sisters were there when our daughter was born and told me how cute she was. They said she had lots of black hair and slept a lot. But I didn't get to see our precious baby girl until she was four days old because I was quite weak from the C-section and I had a terrible, almost non-stop cough.

Little Katie

Katie's weight dropped below five pounds. The doctor told us she couldn't go home until she weighed at least five pounds. For the next seven days, her dad arrived at the hospital promptly at 7 a.m. He came back at 5 p.m. and stayed till 8 p.m. He'd peek in to see me, then go out to the nursery where I'd join him. Sometimes, he joined me at noon for lunch. But he spent most of the time looking at our baby girl.

On the afternoon of the seventh day, we took her home. Dale called her "Little One Eye," as most of the time she slept with one eye half open. Lots of family and friends came to see her. She slept a lot, which concerned me. Also, she rarely finished a four-ounce bottle of her formula. Everyone said, "You are so lucky to have such a good baby!"

Three weeks later, I had just fed her and cleaned her up. Dale held her and I went to see my next-door neighbor. I had barely gotten through door when he called me back. "Karen! I think she's having trouble breathing!"

I hadn't noticed anything wrong, but the look on his face said he was scared. I grabbed the car keys. I told Dale to keep her awake by doing whatever it took. Pinch her, shake her, but keep her awake!

The hospital was seven miles away. We met the doctor there. I told him she slept a lot and didn't finish her formula. He checked her vitals, then hollered at me, "She's not a good baby. She's lazy and starving herself!" Wow.

While Dale drove us home, all I could do was hold her tight and cry. But then things began to turn around.

As our baby began to eat and sleep on a regular schedule, she became a very active child. When she was six months old, we were given a puppy about the same age. It was a lot of work with 2 babies!

My husband had a nice older two story house to care for, but we were all happy. On our property there was a small barn with a young cow in it. Dale took her to see the cow and soon she said "cow." That was her first word! Quite unusual as most kids first say "Mama" or "Dada." Concerned that she might pickup low-toned slurred speech, my doctor and I encouraged Dale to talk and read to her as much as possible. I would play "school" with her. We had books. I'd read to her showing the pictures, then I'd say, "Katie, read now."

A neighbor girl would meet the school bus at our house and would stop to play for a few minutes. I drew a paper clock and put "Margie" by 3:30. Katie soon learned to watch for the bus and say "Margie Here."

Margie was a cheerleader and would demonstrate cheerleading moves for Katie. Soon I found her on the floor moving her arms and legs saying, "Doing like Margie do." Later she was playing with her ABC cards when I said, "Would you like to do your name like Margie does?" I took the 5 letters, spread them out on the table in order, pointing to each and said, "With a K and an A and a T and an I and an E" three times, then "Yay Katie!"

She was always curious about everything, she loved to be outside as much as possible with her dog, and playing golf with her dad. Most of all she liked to be with "Ma," myself and her dad.

Life As a Family

Our baby girl grew up. Katie did well in school, from kindergarten through twelfth grade. From the age of 11 on, she had some kind of job, including pulling weeds in bean fields for many farmers in our area. She loved it. She played trumpet extremely well in the high school band. She also played basketball and golf in high school. During her junior and senior years, she went to the State Golf Tournaments in St. Cloud, Minnesota.

We were so proud of her, especially as she never had private lessons. Her secret? Her dad began coaching her when she was two. Not only was he a very good golf coach, but he made two holes-in-one at the Winthrop, Minnesota Golf Course. Not many men or women have made one hole-in-one. During his lifetime, he was the only person to make two.

When she was 18, our daughter aced the annual Women's Tournament on the same golf course. She beat other golfers who were older and had much more experience. This was a proud and exciting moment for us.

Katie did well in college and learned many different kinds of skills, including welding.

Dale was a very good husband and father. He always said he had four main loves: golf, the kid, the wife, and family. He loved to take Katie with him as he golfed. He was a very complicated man, but a very honest, hard-working one. He was always there for me, especially when I really needed him. The same was true for our daughter.

Dale had some heart trouble in the past. One day, I noticed he didn't seem to be quite his normal self. I asked him, "Are you okay?" He responded, "I'm fine." He seemed to get better and more like himself during the week. Then he told me, "I'm going golfing."

He always said that, if he had his wish, he would like to die on the golf course, just as Bing Crosby had done. In 2000, he got his wish on a beautiful day in May on the fourth hole.

There is much more to tell about Katie's life, but time is short, so this is just my story. Dale has been gone 16 years. Now our family is just the two of us.

I enjoyed teaching for more than 20 years. In 2006, I moved to Litchfield to be close to my daughter.

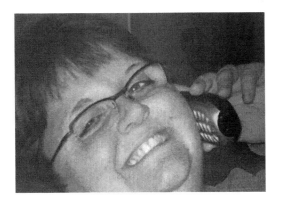

A STORY OF PROGRESS

In 2008, I was appointed to the Housing and Development Authority Board of Litchfield, and in 2010, to the board of directors of Lincoln Apartments, where I live.

Conditions at places like the institution at Redfield are changing. As people have become more knowledgeable, some institutions have been closed down and are no longer being used. Over the years, slowly but surely, I have worked to help improve conditions, watching especially that one place I was most familiar with turn into a greatly improved institution, primarily serving the severely retarded.

Also, we are moving to creating group homes with smaller numbers of residents and have tried to mainstream people into society. It certainly is clear how important it is to correctly diagnose people who are handicapped as I was. I'm a prime example of someone who never should have been placed in such a situation.

Many people have contributed to advances in the treatment of crippled and mentally ill children. Dr. Morrison, during his tenure as director of the new Crippled Children's Hospital and School, raised countless dollars, pioneered many new services, and supervised three building additions. Governor Foss and his wife, June, were also instrumental in making important changes in the treatment of children with special needs.

When I was hired as a Special Education teacher in Gaylord, Minnesota, I worked with the Association for Retarded Citizens and helped develop Sibley County Special Olympics. I also worked at the Arlington Day Activity Center. Because of my work with Governor Foss and my involvement with the Association for Retarded Citizens, the United Cerebral Palsy Association in Sibley County, and various statewide associations, I came to the attention of Minnesota's Governor Perpich.

Governor Perpich adopted the Minnesota State Council for the Developmentally Disabled, which had been started by Governor Joe Foss and others in South Dakota. One day, he called with news that he had appointed me to serve on that board. I did that for six-and-a-half years. That organization is still active, and celebrated its thirty-second anniversary in 2014.

In the 1970s, I gave a live TV interview with Robin Roberts involving a statewide fundraiser for the United Cerebral Palsy Association. I also served for three years on the Minnesota State Board of United Cerebral Palsy and helped start the Council on Aging, which is still very active. The Council on Aging allows those with handicaps to get free rides to their medical appointments. The drivers are volunteers, but they are paid for their mileage. Non-handicapped senior citizens pay a small charge. Ironically, I now use the Council on Aging for rides to out-of-town medical appointments.

DUANE'S STORY:
RETURN TO REDFIELD

My wife and I traveled to Redfield, South Dakota to get a better overall picture of the institution where Karen spent ten years of her life. A lot of things have changed. The most visible changes are many buildings that have been replaced. The number of patients housed there was 1,200 to 1,300. Now there are between 150 and 200. Most importantly, it seems that treatment has improved.

We were fortunate to be able to speak with a man who has worked there since 1970. As we were taking pictures, he stopped and asked us, "Do you have a family member living here?" We told him we knew a lady who had lived here for ten years back in the '40s who had gone on to get her B.S. degree and teach. I remarked I was in the process of writing her biography and planned to publish her story.

He was very interested in hearing more about Karen. He offered to show us around and pointed out various locations Karen had described to us. He told us that in its earlier days, the facility raised its own food — once a common practice in such facilities. It had a dairy herd known to be one of the top herds in the nation. The barns are still standing but are now used for storage.

We asked him about the garden where David had worked. He said, "Follow me and I will show you." We drove over roads marked by signs that said, "For Government Vehicles Only." We passed one of the cemeteries that held patients who were buried in the '40s.

We reached the area that was once the garden, now grown over with grass and trees. It lies next to a river, which once had a bridge that allowed access from the institution. The bridge no longer stands.

The fence that once surrounded the entire complex is gone. Now a short fence marks both sides of the entry into the institution. It appears to be part of the original fence that may have been preserved for historical reasons. For Karen, the fence is a reminder of how much she felt like a caged animal. When I told her the fence was gone, she gave a sigh of relief, and said, "Good."

The grounds looked lovely — nicely landscaped and mowed. It was easy to see why Karen's mom would have felt she was placing David and Karen in a good facility.

Our guide said he would love to have a copy of the book. He also suggested I send a copy to the institution, now called the South Dakota Development Center. I told him that Karen's story is not very complimentary to the institution. He replied, "They realize how things were back then, but there have been huge improvements. I've heard about the horrible treatment that went on with people shackled, but that is all in the past."

I also visited with a young lady who was working at the desk at our motel. I asked whether she was familiar with the development center. Her answer was interesting. "I worked there for a short time, but I did not like working there, so I had to quit." She noted her grandmother had worked there for more than 40 years. (I was hoping her name was not Mrs. B.) I mentioned that some of the people in this book were not very nice. She replied, "It would not have been my grandmother. She treated people like they were her own family." I was glad to hear that.

Other Memories of Redfield

Recently, my wife and I attended a fish fry at a local church in Litchfield. A couple joined us. They said they were not from there, but asked directions to our local Grand Army Hall, which is now a historical museum. We gave them the directions to the Hall, and I proceeded to tell them what a great place it was.

I told them I'm a writer and sometimes do research there for a story. I added that my latest story involved a local woman who had spent ten years in a state hospital in South Dakota.

The husband asked, "What town in South Dakota?" When I said Redfield, he looked shocked and said, "In the '60s, while I was in college, I visited that place. I have never forgotten it."

He talked about a girl, and motioned with his hands to suggest the girl's height. "She was young and only this tall, and she was with these old men who seemed crazy. I've never gotten over it. I couldn't wait to get out of there." The expression on his face showed me and my wife that it was still a very vivid memory, even after all these years.

DUANE'S THOUGHTS

Karen and I spent many hours together as she shared her life story with me. I came to realize how difficult it was for her to revisit so many of the hurts she endured. It's been interesting to see how over time memories have come back that I suspect she had not shared with many other people.

During her childhood, she suffered such isolation and had little communication with the outside world. Mail from her mother was censored, as were Karen's letters home. So it was impossible to tell her mom what she was feeling and what was going on at the institution. To this day, Karen is sensitive about anyone opening her mail.

As an example, she told me this story. Her husband said he had opened some of her mail and found it wasn't anything important. She let him know that nobody opens her mail, not even her husband! If it has her name on it, it is hers to open.

Karen wasn't allowed to acknowledge her brother, David, or any other boys, for that matter. She had no idea why boys, even her own brother, were off limits. She received no sex education so that when her body began to change and she got her period, she had no idea what was going on. She wondered why girls she was living with were taken to the institution's hospital when they were 15 years old. They certainly didn't realize what was going to happen to them. She thinks that had she not been released when she was, she likely would have been sterilized. In my research, I discovered that Redfield was the only place in South Dakota where this was the practice.

I asked Karen if, after being released from Redfield, she'd ever run into Mrs. B. She said, "Once, while I was waiting in Redfield for my bus back to college in Aberdeen, I spotted Mrs. B. at the depot. The memory of her was still strong in my mind. I hoped she wouldn't notice me. But we got on the same bus. Then she moved to my seat and asked, 'Aren't you Karen Huffman?' I said, 'Yes, I am Karen.' Mrs. B. was so friendly and nice, and said, 'I understand you're doing so great.' I would have liked to tell her to get away from me, but I was able to keep my cool and be decent to her. That was a long ride from Redfield to Aberdeen."

Karen shared another incident with me. At one point, her mom went to a family member, a very successful farmer, and asked for a loan to help with the children's medical expenses. She promised to pay back the loan. Her relative said he couldn't help her. Later, Karen went with her mom to visit this relative when he lay on his death bed. He asked her mom to forgive him. Karen's mom replied, "'Til my dying day I will not forgive you." The farmer broke out in tears. Karen said, "I had to leave the room and go outside."

Karen's mother really struggled with her temper, especially after losing David — a loss that affected her whole life. Karen observed her mother over the years and did her best not to be like her. She did not like losing her temper, but felt it helped her to be a survivor. She told me, "If someone mistreats a person I love, like my daughter, I could still lose control. That individual better watch out." With the help of many good friends, teachers, and lots of time, her temper is no longer a problem. In addition, Karen's mom was never one to tell Karen to her face how proud she was of her. She would sometimes tell other people she was proud of her daughter. But Karen longed to hear it from her mother.

The trauma Karen endured during her ten years of imprisonment has been challenging to overcome. It is remarkable that she not only survived that trauma, but overcame it to live a normal life and achieve so much.

I am humbled that she has been willing to share her story with me. And I am humbled that, through this book, she is also willing to share it with you, the reader.

Karen, you are one amazing woman. Thank you for being willing to share your story.

—Duane Hickler

KAREN'S THOUGHTS

For a long time, I felt the odds were against me and nothing was easy. But I have my inborn streak of stubbornness and strong determination to thank for enabling me to accomplish goals that doctors and professors told me I would never reach. Whenever anyone told me I couldn't do something, I'd break my neck trying. I was a real fighter.

But the stubbornness that won me many battles also made me defensive. This was not good. It took me a long time to overcome this defensiveness toward people. I realized it didn't help me or anyone else to be bitter about the past.

For years, I couldn't or wouldn't talk about that part of my life. I certainly never imagined that I would someday stand before audiences of high school seniors or college students and talk about my life in a state institution for the so-called feeble minded. Then it occurred to me that by telling my story, I could help others who were still there.

Along with my determination, I have another quality to be grateful for. I was also able to make friends. My companions in many ways helped me to achieve. One light-hearted example comes from college days. I was required to take a speech course. My assignment was to read a poem aloud. I read it so fast that I got a D-. When the professor told me that was the highest grade I'd get because of my speech handicap, I became very depressed. Then I got creative. The next time I was required to talk, I made a pact with a friend. If I started to talk too fast, she'd wink at me. I was doing fine, glancing at her every so often and growing more confident. For a while, I forgot to look at her. When I finally did, she was winking with both eyes!

Duane Hickler is another friend. He has helped me tell a story I thought I'd never tell. With his patience and willingness to listen, I have been able to talk about difficult things. Without his help, this book would not have become a reality.

I could not, and would not, have done it alone. Thank you, Duane.

Stubbornness and aggressiveness were my earliest defenses against hardship. When I was still very young, I met people who believed in me: kind Dorothy Maskers and the doctor who told me I could accomplish whatever I wanted. Friends like this helped me turn stubbornness into determination, and replace bitterness with a good mental attitude and a positive outlook. When some people told me, "You can't," friends stood by my side as I said, "Watch me!" Thanks to those who influenced me during the toughest years, I learned the value of making friends and having a good sense of humor.

Now my friends jokingly tell me, "Baby, you've come a long way." We sure have.

—*Karen A. Gorr*

APPENDIX A

A Tribute to Governor Foss

Governor Joe Foss was a very important person in my life. For that reason I offer this tribute in recognition of one aspect of his distinguished career: his military service.

Governor Foss had retired to Arizona and was asked to speak at West Point. He thought the cadets would be interested in seeing his Medal of Honor, so he decided to take it with him. He simply slipped it into his pocket. When he tried to board his plane, he was stopped and detained for some time. The screeners finally figured out he was not a threat and let him board the plane with his Medal of Honor still in his pocket.

A World War II hero, Governor Foss received the Congressional Medal of Honor from President Franklin Roosevelt. He was well known for what he accomplished during the war. From October 1942 to November 1942, Captain Foss shot down 23 Japanese planes. He then rose to a Major in the United States Marines, and later to a Brigadier General in the United States Air Force.

Following is a copy of the citation that was read at his Medal of Honor Ceremony:

For outstanding heroism and courage above and beyond the call of duty as executive officer of Marine Fighting Squadron 121, 1ˢᵗ Marine Aircraft Wing at Guadalcanal. Engaging in almost daily combat with the enemy from 9 October to 19 November 1942, Captain Foss personally shot down 23 Japanese planes and damaged others so severely that their destruction was extremely possible. In addition, during this period, he successfully led a large number of escort missions skilfully covering reconnaissance, bombing, and photographic planes as well as surface craft. On 15 January 1943 he added 3 more enemy planes to his already brilliant success for a record of aerial combat achievement unsurpassed in this war. Boldly searching out an approaching enemy force on 25 January, Captain Foss led his 8 F-4F Marine planes and 4 Army P-38s into action and, undaunted by tremendously superior numbers, intercepted and struck with such force that 4 Japanese fighters were shot down and the bombers were turned back without releasing a single bomb. His remarkable flying skill, inspiring leadership, and indomitable fighting spirit were distinctive factors in the defense of strategic American positions on Guadalcanal.

APPENDIX B

Timeline: The Path to Progress for People with Physical Disabilities

Karen A. Gorr was born in Monte Vista, Colorado in 1937. Her brother, David, was born two years earlier. Both of them were born healthy but developed physical challenges early in life.

Karen's disabilities were caused by a childhood illness, while David suffered an injury that led to seizures. David passed away when he was 13. Karen has lived to see tremendous progress on the path to civil rights for people with physical disabilities.

Beginning in 1940, Karen and David were placed in the State School and Home for the Feeble Minded in Redfield, South Dakota. This was a residential facility for people of all ages where patients suffered abuse and neglect at the hands of uncaring employees.

In 2016, the institution where Karen and David were incarcerated still exists. It is now called the South Dakota Development Center. However, it's gone from warehousing between 1,200 to 1,300 patients in 1940 to providing a safe home for a far smaller, and happier, group of between 150 and 200 patients.

A man who has worked at the institution since the 1970s and now acts as a guide was happy to hear about Karen's memoir even though he knew it was critical of the institution as it was in the 1940s. In fact, he even requested a copy of the book.

He said, of the South Dakota Development Center, "They realize how things were back then, but there have been huge improvements. I've heard about the horrible treatment that went on with people shackled, but that is all in the past."

So between 1940 and 2016, there's been a sea change for people with disabilities that's evident in the place where Karen spent so much of her childhood. Here are some of the milestones for all people with physical disabilities that Karen has witnessed in her lifetime:

- 1948. Dr. Howard A. Rusk establishes the Rusk Institute of Rehabilitation Medicine in New York City. He focuses on the emotional, psychological and social aspects of individuals with disabilities so that he can treat World War II veterans. This lays the foundation for modern rehabilitation medicine.

- 1950s. People with disabilities begin the barrier-free movement. The Veterans Administration, President's Committee on Employment of the Handicapped, the National Easter Seals Society, and other groups work together to develop national standards for "barrier-free" buildings.

- 1961. The American Standards Association, later known as the American National Standards Institute (ANSI), publishes Making Buildings Accessible to and Usable by the Physically Handicapped. This creates standards for enabling people with disabilities to get into, and use, classrooms, offices, lobbies, hotel rooms, and so forth. It applies to remodeling existing buildings and to new constructions.

- 1965. Medicaid Help for Low-Income and Disabled Title XIX (19) of the Social Security Act is created and establishes Medicaid. This federal/state entitlement program pays medical costs for low-income people with disabilities.

- 1973. Section 504 of the 1973 Rehabilitation Act is passed. This makes it illegal for federal agencies, public universities, and other public institutions receiving any federal funds to discriminate against people with disabilities and establishes their civil rights. For the first time, it is prohibited to exclude and segregate people because of their disabilities. Their educational and workplace challenges are no longer seen as inevitable. Now, those challenges theoretically are illegal if they are caused by discriminatory policies and practices. In practice, Section 504 isn't always honored, though.

• 1975. The Education for All Handicapped Children Act is passed to guarantee equal access to public education for children with disabilities. This gives every child, including children with disabilities, the right to a full education in mainstream classes.

• 1978. The National Council on Disability is established as a Department of Education advisory board to guarantee equal opportunity for all people with disabilities, enable them to live independently and become self sufficient, and participate fully in society.

• 1979. The first test of Section 504 results in disappointment. The Supreme Court decides the case of Southeastern Community College v. Davis. The Court deems Frances Davis, who is hearing-impaired, to be unfit to attend Southeastern Community College because she wouldn't be able to fulfill its clinical requirements. More work clearly is needed to protect people with disabilities.

• 1980. The Civil Rights of Institutionalized Persons Act (CRIPA) is passed to give the Department of Justice power to sue institutions that violate the rights of disabled people who are being held as in-patients against their will.

• 1986. The Air Carrier Access Act is passed to require airlines to provide disabled people with boarding access and certain accessibility features in new or remodeled airports.

• 1987. The Supreme Court decides the case of School Board of Nassau County v. Arline. Gene Arline was fired (without a financial settlement in her favor) as an elementary school because she had tuberculosis which was a recurring contagious disease. Arline asked for protection under the Rehabilitation Act of 1973, saying that the school had fired her because of her illness which was a handicap. A federal district court decided that having tuberculosis did not make Arline handicapped, but the Supreme Court overtruns that decision. It declares that Arline is handicapped, and this paves the way for AIDs patients to be protected under Section 504 as well.

• 1988. The Fair Housing Act (FHA) is amended to included protection for the disabled under the civil rights statute that banning race discrimination in housing.

• 1989. The Americans With Disabilities Act (ADA) is introduced in the 101st Congress to prohibit discrimination of people with disabilities in the workplace, public services, and public accommodations.

- 1990. The Americans with Disabilities Act (ADA) is passed. Also, the Education for All Handicapped Children Act of 1975 is renamed the Individuals with Disabilities Education Act (IDEA). This elaborates on the rights of disabled children and focuses on the rights of their parents to be involved in the educational decisions that affect their children. It requires that parents have the opportunity to approve an Individual Education Plan that's designed to meet the educational needs of their disabled children.

- 1992. Title III of the Americans with Disabilities Act (ADA) allows people with disabilities to have equal access to public accommodations and commercial facilities including schools, restaurants, doctors' offices, and the like.

- 1996. The Telecommunications Act is passed and gives disabled people access to computers, telephones, closed captioning, and many other telecommunication devices.

- The first Disability Pride Parade is held in Chicago. Almost 2,000 people attend (which is about 4 times the number of people who were expected).

- A first-of-its-kind bill requires public school students from kindergarten through twelfth grade to learn the history of the disability rights movement.

APPENDIX C

Resources

When Karen A. Gorr and her older brother, David, lost their father in 1940, they were placed by their mother in the State School and Home for the Feeble Minded in Redfield, South Dakota. There, they were neglected, emotionally and physically abused, inadequately fed, and only minimally educated.

If there had been more options available to disabled people at the time, Karen's mother may well have tapped into those resources to provide a better life for her children. That opportunity is gone forever for Karen.

The good news is that, since that dark time in Karen's life, the public has overwhelmingly demanded change and civil rights for people who are disabled. A host of resources has been created to enhance the lives of disabled individuals. Here are a few to get started. All of the institutions listed below also have Web sites.

Administration for Community Living

An arm of the U.S. Department of Health and Human Services, the Administration for Community acts as an online clearinghouse for resources designed to help individuals with disabilities.

ADDRESS:
Administration for Community Living
330 C St SW
Washington, DC 20201

PHONE NUMBERS:
Administration for Community Living:
(202) 401-4634

Eldercare Locator (to find local resources):
(800) 677-1116

EMAIL:
Requests for information about ACL programs and comments can be sent to: aclinfo@acl.hhs.gov

Association of People Supporting Employment First

This advocacy group facilitates the full inclusion of people with disabilities in the workplace and the community.

ADDRESS:
414 Hungerford Drive
Sappen, MD 20850

PHONE:
(301) 279-0060

EMAIL:
membership@apse.org or communications@apse.org

Center for Disabilities, University of South Dakota

History of the Disability Movement in South Dakota

Article: "From 'Imbecile, Idiot, Feeble Minded to People First' 150 Years of Struggle" by Thomas E. Scheinost

Request by email: cd@usd.edu

Center for Parent Information and Resources

This is a hub of information for parents of adults with disabilities.

ADDRESS:
Center for Parent Information and Resources
c/o Statewide Parent Advocacy Network
35 Halsey St., Fourth Floor
Newark, NJ 07102

Disability Resources on the Internet

A guide to organizations that provide services to disabled people.

ADDRESS:
Disability Resources, inc.
Dept. IN, Four Glatter Lane
Centereach, NY 11720-1032 USA

PHONE:
(631) 585-0290, weekdays from 9 a.m. to 5 p.m. EST

EMAIL:
info@disabilityresources.org

Easterseals

Established nearly 100 years ago, Easterseals has been helping individuals with disabilities and special needs, and their families, live better lives.

ADDRESS:
One Concorde Gate, Suite 700
Toronto, ON   M3C 3N6

PHONE:
(416) 421-8377
(800) 668-6252

EMAIL:
info@easterseals.org

United States Federal Government

The U.S. Federal Government provides a web site (disability.gov) that offers information on disability programs and services nationwide.

ACKNOWLEDGMENTS

A kind, motherly woman named Dorothy Maskers, a patient in the ward where I spent 10 years of my life, was very special to me. She taught me and other children how to read, print, and play Parcheesi. Dorothy took me under her wing.

Dr. Morrison, Director of the new Crippled Children's Hospital and School, raised countless dollars, pioneered many new services, and supervised three building additions. As one who initially thought I'd never graduate from high school, he later told me he was proud of me, and said, "Keep up the good work."

Former Governor of South Dakota Joe Foss and his wife, June, were important in my life. I lived with them in the Governor's Mansion from my sophomore through senior years of high school.

The Dean of Northern State College in Aberdeen, South Dakota, believed in me when my advisor didn't. (She said I didn't walk well enough or talk plain enough.) The Dean recommended physical therapy and a speech therapist. After months of therapy, they interviewed me, and the Dean said, "Karen, you did wonderfully in here. Go finish your degree and teach." This support was key in the completing my Bachelor of Science degree in Special Education.

My college roommate, Connie, became a special friend. She was the first black person I'd ever met. Connie and I had something in common. It was easy enough to see that I had a disability. I walked with a slight limp, and sometimes had problems speaking clearly. The prejudice she suffered in school was her "disability." When she took me home to Des Moines to meet her family, they treated me as if I were part of their family.

Last but not least, this book simply would not exist without the encouragement and generosity of Duane's nephew, Steven "Cash" Nickerson, President and a Principal of PDS Tech, Inc., and founder of CNM Press.

In addition to bringing my story to the world, he is a proud supporter of the Siteman Cancer Center, dedicated to helping find a cure for prostate cancer. He also received the Global Philanthropy Award in 2010 from Washington University in St. Louis for his support of the Crimes Against Humanity Initiative.

ABOUT THE AUTHOR
AND COLLABORATOR

Karen Gorr was born on April 6, 1937. When she was six months old, she was stricken with rickets. She then developed cerebral palsy. Karen's father died when she was three. The same year, Karen and her five year old brother, David, were admitted to an institution. David died in the institution from pneumonia.

Ten years later, Karen's mom took her to live with her in Pierre, South Dakota where Karen learned to walk, started school at age 13 in the third grade, and completed high school in 1958. She entered Northern State College's Special Education Program, completing two internships: one for Mentally Handicapped and one for the Physically Handicapped K through 12. She then completed Student Teaching. She went on to teach for 20 years at the high school level.

Collaborator Duane Hickler received his education at Litchfield High School in Litchfield, Minnesota and

Olivet Nazarene College in Kankakee, Illinois. He farmed for 25 years and then became a district sales manager for an agriculture company that sold corn and soybean seed. Writing is one of his major passions in life.

66519725R00067

Made in the USA
Lexington, KY
16 August 2017